Date: 02/15/12

**E SCHAEFER**
**Schaefer, Lola M.,**
**A rainy day /**

# A Rainy Day

by Lola M. Schaefer

Consulting Editor: Gail Saunders-Smith, Ph.D.

Consultant: Chris S. Orr, Certified Consulting Meteorologist, American Meteorological Society

## Pebble Books

an imprint of Capstone Press
Mankato, Minnesota

Pebble Books are published by Capstone Press,
151 Good Counsel Drive, P.O. Box 669, Mankato, Minnesota 56002.
www.capstonepress.com

*Library of Congress Cataloging-in-Publication Data*
Schaefer, Lola M., 1950–
    A rainy day/by Lola M. Schaefer.
    p. cm.—(What kind of day is it?)
    Includes bibliographical references and index.
    Summary: Simple text and photographs depict a rainy day, including the
formation of rain and the actions of the people out in it.
    ISBN-10: 0-7368-0404-8 (hardcover)
    ISBN-13: 978-07368-0404-2 (hardcover)
    ISBN-10: 0-7368-8622-2 (paperback)
    ISBN-13: 978-0-7368-8622-2 (paperback)
    1. Rain and rainfall—Juvenile literature. 2. Raindrops—Juvenile literature.
[1. Rain and rainfall.] I. Title. II. Series.
QC924.7.S3  2000
551.57'7—dc21
            99-18355
            CIP

# Note to Parents and Teachers

The series What Kind of Day Is It? supports national science standards for units on basic features of the earth. The series also shows that short-term weather conditions can change daily. This book describes and illustrates what happens on a rainy day. The photographs support emergent readers in understanding the text. The repetition of words and phrases helps emergent readers learn new words. This book also introduces emergent readers to subject-specific vocabulary words, which are defined in the Words to Know section. Emergent readers may need assistance to read some words and to use the Table of Contents, Words to Know, Read More, Internet Sites, and Index/Word List sections of the book.

012011
006038VMI

# Table of Contents

Today is a rainy day.

Rain forms in clouds.

8

Rain falls from clouds.

Rain brings water to rivers, lakes, and oceans.

Rain brings water
to plants.

14

Rain brings water
to animals.

People carry umbrellas on a rainy day.

People splash in puddles
on a rainy day.

20

Rainbows appear
on a rainy day.

# Words to Know

**appear**—to come into sight

**cloud**—a white or gray mass of water droplets and dust in the air; raindrops form in certain types of clouds.

**puddle**—a small pool of water; puddles often collect on the ground after it rains.

**rainbow**—an arc of colors in the sky; rainbows form when sunlight shines through water droplets in the air; the colors in a rainbow include red, orange, yellow, green, blue, indigo, and violet.

**umbrella**—a frame with cloth stretched over it; umbrellas protect people from rain; people can fold umbrellas when they are not using them.

# Read More

**Burton, Jane and Kim Taylor.** *The Nature and Science of Rain.* Exploring the Science of Nature. Milwaukee: Gareth Stevens, 1997.

**Owen, Andy and Miranda Ashwell.** *Rain.* What Is Weather? Des Plaines, Ill.: Heinemann Library, 1999.

**Saunders-Smith, Gail.** *Rain.* Weather. Mankato, Minn.: Pebble Books, 1998.

# Internet Sites

FactHound offers a safe, fun way to find Internet sites related to this book. All of the sites on FactHound have been researched by our staff.

Here's how:

1. Visit *www.facthound.com*
2. Type in this special code **0736804048** for age-appropriate sites. Or enter a search word related to this book for a more general search.
3. Click on the **Fetch It** button.

FactHound will fetch the best sites for you!

# Index/Word List

animals, 15
appear, 21
brings, 11, 13, 15
carry, 17
clouds, 7, 9
day, 5, 17, 19, 21
falls, 9
forms, 7
lakes, 11
oceans, 11
people, 17, 19

plants, 13
puddles, 19
rain, 7, 9, 11, 13, 15
rainbows, 21
rainy, 5, 17, 19, 21
rivers, 11
splash, 19
today, 5
umbrellas, 17
water, 11, 13, 15

**Word Count: 52**
**Early-Intervention Level: 6**

**Editorial Credits**
Martha E. H. Rustad, editor; Abby Bradford, Bradfordesign, Inc., cover designer;
    Heidi Schoof, photo researcher

**Photo Credits**
Index Stock Imagery, cover, 20; Index Stock Imagery/Grafica, 1
J. Lotter/TOM STACK & ASSOCIATES, 16
Joe McDonald/TOM STACK & ASSOCIATES, 12
Richard Hamilton Smith, 18
Robert McCaw, 6, 8, 10
Uniphoto/Donald A. Katchusky, 4
Visuals Unlimited/Rob Simpson, 14